Boise State University Western Writers Series Number 16

Frederic Remington

By Fred Erisman
Texas Christian University

A portion of this work, in altered form, has appeared in the *South Dakota Review.*

Editors: Wayne Chatterton
James H. Maguire

Business Manager:
James Hadden

Cover Illustration by Frederic Remington, Courtesy of The Amon Carter Museum of Western Art, Fort Worth, Texas

Boise State University, Boise, Idaho

Library of Congress Card No. 75-7009

International Standard Book No. 0-88430-015-3

Printed in the United States of America by
The Caxton Printers, Ltd.
Caldwell, Idaho

REVIEW COPIES
(5)

Frederic Remington

Frederic Remington

To an entire generation of readers, Frederic Remington was the spokesman for the American West. For almost a quarter of a century, from 1886 until his death in 1909, his drawings and paintings, published in *Harper's Weekly, The Century, Harper's New Monthly Magazine, Collier's,* and other large-circulation magazines of the time, gave to many readers their only glimpses of Western life and the western landscape. The popular acclaim for his work was echoed by the American art establishment. During his lifetime, Remington was elected to membership in the National Academy of Design and awarded an honorary Bachelor of Fine Arts by Yale University; in his last years his paintings and bronzes were exhibited and sold by Tiffany's and Knoedler's, two of the most prestigious of New York firms. In the years following his death, his stature grew still greater. Three major museums, the Amon Carter Museum of Western Art in Fort Worth, Texas; the Thomas Gilcrease Institute of American History and Art in Tulsa, Oklahoma; and the Remington Art Museum in Ogdensburg, New York, feature extensive collections of his works, while smaller holdings can be found in museums from the Smithsonian Institution to the Whitney Museum in Cody, Wyoming.

And yet, although Remington the painter and sculptor needs little introduction, Remington the author is virtually unknown. Despite a writing career that began with journalism in the 1880's and gave rise to eight books by 1906, he remains known almost exclusively as a pictorial artist. His paintings, such as "A Dash for the Timber" or "A Cavalryman's Breakfast on the Plains," are commonplaces. Conversely, the very titles of his books are unfamiliar, and the number of persons who can claim a first-hand acquaintance with *Sundown Leflare* (1889), *John Ermine of the Yellowstone* (1902), or *The Way of an Indian* (1906) is infinitesimal. The recent reprintings of *Pony Tracks* (1895), *Crooked Trails* (1898), and *John Ermine* make a selection of his writings accessible to the student. But Remington the author remains obscure.

That Remington's writings are largely overshadowed by his paintings is understandable but unfortunate, for his books are a significant complement to his paintings in developing his view of the West. His attempts to record in his paintings a West that was vanishing under the wheels of industrial progress are well known. In his books, however, he expands this recording, adding to it his sense of what the West had been, and his recognition of what its passing had cost American life. As he unveils his gallery of scouts, soldiers, Indians, and cowpunchers, he communicates a sense of time and place that can stand unashamedly alongside that given by his paintings and bronzes.

Frederic Sackrider Remington was born in Canton, New York, on October 4, 1861, the only child of Clara Sackrider and Seth Pierpont Remington. His parents, married in January of that year, were well known in the community. Clara was the daughter of one of the prominent families of Canton; and Seth, a loyal Republican, had some years earlier founded the *St. Lawrence Plaindealer,* a weekly newspaper of Republican leaning that he edited and published.

Young Remington saw little of his father during his early years. Commissioned as a captain in the Union forces in the summer of 1862, Seth served first in Washington, then in Louisiana, Mississippi, and Arkansas. By the end of the Civil War, he had been promoted to major. After the war, Seth resumed his career as a journalist in Bloomington, Illinois, returning to Canton in 1867. In 1870, his work for the Republican Party won him an appointment as United States Collector of the Port of Ogdensburg, New York, a post that he held until his death in 1880. For the Remington family, Ogdensburg became home.

Seth's military experience left its mark on Frederic, whose early schooling was erratic. In 1875 he spent a year at the Vermont Episcopal Institute. This arrangement suited no one, and in 1876, at Seth's insistence, he was enrolled in Highland Military Academy at Worcester, Massachusetts. After two years here, which, from all accounts, he enjoyed, Remington entered Yale University in the fall of 1878, but he was not particularly happy at Yale. The art curriculum he found dull. Football, under the leadership of Walter Camp, was more to his taste. He did not, though, have time to develop either pursuit. His second year at Yale was interrupted by his father's illness, and when Seth died on February 10, 1880, Frederic decided not to return to the university.

For the next two years Remington drifted, making a brief summer trip to Montana in 1881, and then working as a clerk for the New York state government in Albany. In October 1882, on his twenty-first birthday, he received a patrimony of slightly more than $4,000. Promptly resigning his clerkship, he left for Kansas, where he bought a half-section of land and began a sheep ranch in the spring of 1883. Here his devotion to the West began to develop. He got a taste of Western high-jinks while drinking and rabbit-hunting with friends. He also took a lengthy trip on horseback through the Indian and New Mexico territories, gaining a new respect for the landscape. A distaste for the routine work of the ranch, combined with a drop in the price of wool, ended the venture in May 1884. He sold the ranch and moved to Kansas City.

His marriage on October 1, 1884, to Eva ("Missie") Caten, a Canton girl, forced a change. After a continuing series of financial setbacks, the Remingtons left Kansas and moved to New York City, where Frederic began classes at the Art Students League and attempted to eke out a living doing magazine illustrations. Although he had had a drawing published in redrawn form in *Harper's Weekly* in 1882, he did not make a major sale until 1886. Then, in three years of intensive work, he quickly established himself as an illustrator and journalist. His essays in *Harper's Weekly* and *The Century* gave evidence of his developing talent as a writer, while a silver medal from the Paris Universal Exposition of 1889 and the hanging of "A Dash for the Timber" by the National Academy of Design confirmed his growing reputation as a painter.

The decade from 1890 to 1900 was one of almost continual triumph. He moved to New Rochelle, New York, in the spring of 1890, but he spent the fall in South Dakota and Montana, gathering material under commission from *Harper's.* He was elected an associate member of the National Academy of Design in 1891. In 1892 he was commissioned to illustrate a new edition of Francis Parkman's *The Oregon Trail,* and he spent part of the summer traveling in Europe and Africa with Poultney Bigelow. He held his first one-man show in 1893, at the gallery of the American Art Association, and gave over part of the summer of 1894 to a hunting trip in the Dakotas, returning to report the Chicago railroad riots for the Harper magazines. In 1895 he produced his first bronze, "The Bronco Buster," a significant achievement in itself, then followed it in 1896 with the even more striking "The Wounded Bunkie." An abortive excursion to Cuba with Richard Harding Davis in December of 1896 prepared the way for his more protracted stay in 1898, when he served as a correspondent with the United States forces in the Spanish-American War. The summer of 1899 found him traveling through Montana and Wyoming, once again in search of Western materials. In 1900 he received formal academic recognition for his work when Yale University awarded him an honorary Bachelor of Fine Arts degree.

The pace of these years is reflected in the rapid increase of his literary production. In addition to his numerous exhibitions, he published portfolios and books of his drawings, and began to collect his writings for book publication. *Pony Tracks,* his first, was a collection of essays previously published in the Harper magazines. *Crooked Trails,* which followed, continued the format, while *Stories of Peace and War* (1899) reprinted three stories already published in the first two books. In *Sundown Leflare* he showed signs of attempting a sustained narrative, but *Men With the Bark On* (1900) combined a scattering of Western stories with dispatches from Cuba in the way that had become familiar by this time.

After the turn of the century, Remington slowed his pace somewhat, attempting to perfect his skills as painter, author, and sculptor. His last years were ones of security and experimentation. In 1903 he negotiated a contract with *Collier's* that gave the magazine exclusive rights to twelve new paintings each year in return for an annual salary of $10,000 for himself. Freed from the necessity of taking pot-boiling commissions, Remington blossomed. His paintings took on a distinctly impressionistic look. His sculptures became more and more venturesome, culminating in the precariously balanced "The Outlaw" of 1906 and in the graceful "Trooper of the Plains, 1868" of 1909. Moreover, with *John Ermine of the Yellowstone* and *The Way of an Indian,* his writings at last bore out the promise of the earlier works. When he died on December 26, 1909, of complications following surgery for a ruptured appendix, he was at the height of his creative powers.

In all of his works, Remington is first of all a story-teller. Helen Card, the author of several brief studies of his work, remarks that "subject was everything to Remington, and with him techniques and theories were properly only means to help him tell his story" (*Pony Tracks,* 1961 edn., p. xvii). The story that he tells, in his writings as in his paintings, is that of the vanishing West—a West of changing locales, changing people, and changing ways of life, as seen by one who was present at the end of the "Old West." In 1905, reminiscing about his maiden trip to the West, he writes:

> I knew the railroad was coming—I saw men already swarming into the land. I knew the derby hat, the smoking chimneys, the cord-binder, and the thirty-day note were upon us in a resistless surge. I knew the wild riders and the vacant land were about to vanish forever, and the more I considered the subject the bigger the Forever loomed. . . . I saw the living, breathing end of three American centuries of smoke and dust and sweat, and I now see quite another thing where it all took place, but it does not appeal to me. ("A Few Words from Mr. Remington," p. 16)

The nostalgic perspective that he reveals in this late passage develops slowly throughout his writings.

The regard for factual detail that Remington shows in his paintings is reflected in his early reportorial writings. Coming into writing from a well-established career as an illustrator, he began, not surprisingly, as a reporter, publishing straightforward journalistic articles in *The Century* and *Harper's Weekly.* His first book, *Pony Tracks,* is a selective collection taken from the more than three dozen pieces he had done for the Harper magazines before 1895. Published in April 1895, *Pony Tracks* comprises fifteen essays falling into three general categories: accounts of hunting and fishing expeditions, vignettes of ranching in Mexico, and reports of military activities of various sorts.

The three sporting essays are "Black Water and Shallows," relating a canoe trip in the North Woods; "Stubble and Slough in Dakota," an account of a bird-hunting expedition to the

Dakotas; and "Bear-Chasing in the Rocky Mountains," a vivid description of a bear hunt. In these pieces, Remington establishes his love for the outdoors and for the camaraderie of the hunting party. Freely admitting his own status as a greenhorn in the woods or on the prairies, he describes the hunt in admiring terms, acknowledging the ability of those who are skillful with gun, paddle, or axe. As an outsider who is gradually learning the ropes, he takes a romantic view of the experience. Unknown difficulties merely add to the zest, and the combination of physical exertion and natural beauty leads him in times of rest to "loll back on [his] pack. . . . moralize, and think thoughts which have dignity" (*Pony Tracks,* p. 88). In the ritual fellowship of the trail he finds a substantial quality already missing from city life. This quality, dignified competence, permits a high degree of self-reliance. In his later works, he writes about this quality in other contexts.

Somewhat more significant than the sporting essays are the four descriptions of Mexican ranch life, "An Outpost of Civilization," "A Rodeo at Los Ojos," "In the Sierra Madre with the Punchers," and "Coaching in Chihuahua." Although he writes as the artist in search of material, always looking for a vivid piece of local color or a striking landscape, Remington makes plain his belief that the harshness of ranch life produces a special and admirable human being. This person is the cowboy, a character he had already made familiar through his pictorial works. Ranch life he sees as straightforward, involving many of the same skills required for the hunt. The life is also chancy, one in which the threat of sudden death is strikingly real. Out of this mode of existence comes a person well equipped to confront the demands of daily life:

> In any association with these men of the frontier I have come to greatly respect their moral fibre and their character. Modern civilization, in the process of educating men beyond their capacity, often succeeds in vulgarizing

> them; but these natural men possess minds which, though lacking all embellishments, are chaste and simple, and utterly devoid of a certain flippancy which passes for smartness in situations where life is not so real. (*Pony Tracks,* pp. 61-62)

Here, as in the hunting essays, he conveys his admiration for the person who deals directly, simply, and competently with any problem that confronts him.

This admiration undergirds Remington's regard for the military, for nowhere, he believes, is straightforward competence so nearly perfected as in the United States Army. He presents eight accounts of military life: "Chasing a Major-General," "Lieutenant Casey's Last Scout," "The Sioux Outbreak in South Dakota," "Policing the Yellowstone," "A Model Squadron," "The Affair of the --th of July," "The Colonel of the First Cycle Infantry," and "A Merry Christmas in a Sibley Teepee." Throughout these essays, he consistently praises the Army, having no patience with those who would dilute its professionalism or weigh it down with muddle-headed restrictions. Augustus Thomas, the playwright, summed up Remington's position with the observation that the author-illustrator "loathed all politicians because they talked. He loved the soldiers because the military acted promptly and without debate. In his day in the West the local advent of troopers meant sudden and inflexible order. He saw humanity's future safe only under military discipline" (*The Print of My Remembrance,* p. 336). Remington's own comments reinforce Thomas's summary. Cavalrymen are "a homogeneous class whom we all know. . . . They are punctilious; they respect forms, and always do the dignified and proper thing at the particular instant, and never display their individuality except on two occasions: one is the field of battle and the other is before breakfast" (*Pony Tracks,* p. 13). Discipline, dignity, and directness identify the soldier; their absence marks all that Remington dislikes.

The range of his dislikes is plain from his early treatment of the Indian and his reports of the Chicago riots of 1894. The Indian, as presented in this first book, is brutal, dishonest, and depraved, a totally animalistic being. "The Sioux Outbreak in South Dakota" is tinged with Remington's regret at not having witnessed the encounter at Wounded Knee, and "Lieutenant Casey's Last Scout" rings with indignation at the bleeding hearts in Washington whose sentimental concern for savages has sent a promising young officer to his death. His sympathies are with the Army, and he wastes no love on either the Indian or the bureaucrat.

These sympathies he extends in "The Affair of the --th of July" and "The Colonel of the First Cycle Infantry," two ventures into fiction based upon his experiences reporting the 1894 Pullman strike riots. In both pieces of writing, Remington's disgust toward those who break the law is obvious, as is his respect for the military men who strive to enforce the law. The first story takes the form of a letter from a military aide who has witnessed the Chicago disturbances. He calls the strikers anarchists and toughs, and speaks admiringly of the methodical way in which the Army breaks down their opposition. It closes with a characteristically direct statement: "Chicago is thoroughly worked up now, and if they keep with the present attention to detail, they will have a fine population left" (*Pony Tracks,* p. 144). The second story continues in this vein. A tongue-in-cheek tale told with unsettling blandness, it relates a conversation between Major Ladigo of the cavalry and Colonel Pedal of the bicycle infantry. They discuss the most effective way of putting down a citizen revolt, and although neither is willing to concede the efficacy of his particular unit, both agree that any means of suppressing such a revolt is worthy. There is no doubt that, to Remington, the soldier with his clear-cut sense of purpose and his regard for what is proper is preferable to either the "animalistic savage" or the "irresponsible" citizen. This belief clearly relates to Remington's praise of self-reliance in the hunting essays and persists in his later works, though it undergoes some modification.

Uneven though it is in the mixture of its contents, *Pony Tracks* marks Remington's literary debut, establishing a starting point for his literary development. He is, at this time, very much the reporter, selectively recording what passes in front of him and evaluating it against the standards that he holds at the time. Sometimes the greenhorn, sometimes the admiring participant, and always the perceptive observer, he sets down his reactions to the world as he meets it. In his later works he will modify these reactions. He will expand his vision to embrace the past as well as the present, he will acknowledge the changing status of the Indian, and he will record a much more complex view of human society. In this early work, however, he is concerned solely with the present, striving to set it down with the simple directness that he also admires.

The three years between 1895, when *Pony Tracks* appeared, and 1898, when his second book, *Crooked Trails,* was published, were busy ones for Remington. The period was an artistically rich one, as he perfected his skills in bronze and maintained a heavy load of commissions for paintings and illustrations. He also developed his literary skills, as he kept up a steady flow of journalism, experimented with a variety of narrative techniques, and grew in stature and reputation as a writer as well as an artist.

The volume of his work during these years, combined with the development of his story-telling talents, attracted considerable public attention. In 1897, responding to Remington's comments on his own work, Theodore Roosevelt, then Assistant Secretary of the Navy, wrote to him:

> Are you aware, O sea-going plainsman, that aside from what you do with the pencil, you come closer to the real thing with the pen than any other man in the western business? And I include Hough, Grinnell and Wister. Your articles have been a growing surprise. I don't know how you do it, any more than I know how Kipling does it; but somehow you get close not only to the plainsman and soldier, but to the half-breed and Indian, in the same way Kipling does to the British Tommy and the Gloucester codfisher. Literally innumerable short stories and sketches of cowboys, Indians and soldiers have been, and will be written. Even if very good they will die like mushrooms, unless they are the very best; but the very best will live and will make the cantos in the last Epic of the Western Wilderness before it ceased being a wilderness. Now, I think you are writing this 'very best.' (*Letters of Theodore Roosevelt,* ed. Elting E. Morrison, *et al.,* I, 749)

Roosevelt's estimate, with its characteristic vigor, reveals Remington's growing literary strength in this period. Clear-cut in their factual detail, his articles and short stories now bring to the reader a growing sense of the changes taking place in Western life.

Crooked Trails, like *Pony Tracks* a collection of short pieces taken from the Harper magazines, continues the model established by the earlier work, featuring stories of hunting, Western local color, and military exploits. Unlike *Pony Tracks,* however, it is a clear step forward in Remington's artistic development; it reveals his growing concern with national affairs, his increasing awareness of the past, and his tempering of his earlier views toward the Indian.

The two hunting tales, "The Blue Quail of the Cactus" and "The Strange Days That Came to Jimmie Friday," are unembellished, dryly humorous accounts of mankind's confrontations with nature. The former, in which Remington again appears as the naive greenhorn, relates a quail hunting trip into Mexico, providing an opportunity for him to poke fun at his own Easternized clothing and to describe the discomforts he found in a patch of prickly-pear cactus. The latter tale tells of three greenhorns and their canoeing expedition into Canada. It gains in ironic impact through Remington's contrasting of the campers' reactions to the Canadian wilderness with those of Jimmie Friday, their bemused Indian guide and cook.

Of the three stories of Western life, two are comparatively slight. These are "Cracker Cowboys of Florida," a dismal picture of the amoral, marginally competent drovers of the palmetto forests—a pointed contrast to his earlier, admiring picture of Mexican cowboys—and "The Soledad Girls," an appreciation of the earthy and unaffected wife and daughters of a rancher in Mexico. The third story, "How the Law Got Into the Chaparral," which opens the book, is more substantial. An interview with the aging Colonel Rip Ford of the Texas Rangers, it affords Remington another opportunity to praise directness and competence as he talks of the Rangers' ideals and of their courage under fire. In this context, he speaks of "the brave young faces of the hosts which poured into Texas to war with the enemies of their race . . . impelled by Destiny to conquer, like their remote ancestors, 'the godless hosts of Pagan' who 'came swimming o'er the Northern Sea' " (*Crooked Trails,* 1969 ed., p. 2). His respect for bravery is plain. Equally plain, as Ben M. Vorpahl points out, is his drawing of a parallel between events in Texas in the 1830's, described in this passage, and the increasingly tense international situation of his own times (*My Dear Wister,* p. 220). Remington's yearning for direct action and his skepticism toward all peoples but his own reach their fullest development in his later reports of the Spanish-American War.

The same attitudes appear in the three military stories of *Crooked Trails.* "The Essentials at Fort Adobe" is Remington writing as a straightforward journalist, recording several days of cavalry sorties against the Indians and stressing the vigor, reliability, and workaday competence of the frontier soldier. "Massai's Crooked Trail" continues the commonplace view of the Indian as savage, telling of an Apache warrior's depredations throughout Arizona. Though he portrays Massai as an unregenerate savage, Remington cannot help taking a certain pride in the warrior's singlehanded resistance to his pursuers. The third story, "A Sergeant of the Orphan Troop," moves from the Indian to the soldier, focusing upon Sergeant Carter Johnson of the Third Cavalry. Here Remington ceases to be the reporter and becomes the overt mythologizer. Ruthless with the Cheyenne warrior of Nebraska, gentle with an orphaned Indian child, and possessed of exceptional personal courage and resourcefulness, Johnson emerges as the typical soldier of the American West. He is a person of considerable ability, but he is brought to his present state of competence mostly because he has been toughened and honed by the military life. The message is plain: good men are made better by a demanding existence.

The two remaining stories of the collection are in many ways the most significant, for they show Remington's experimentation with ways of telling a story, and they suggest the beginnings of an important development in his attitude toward the Indian. Both stories purport to be historical documents that Remington has edited. He speaks in them only as the frame narrator, letting the voices from the past carry the burden of the narrative. "Joshua Goodenough's Old Letter," the more readable of the two, since Remington avoids the archaic spellings and long esses of the other, is a historically detailed account of life with Rogers' Rangers in the 1750's, told by one of their scouts in a letter to his son. Writing in his old age, Goodenough makes clear the special skills needed to survive in the forests of New

York, the hardships worked by the wilderness upon the unprepared and therefore incompetent British regulars, and the consistent faithfulness with which he has done his duty.

More difficult and more revealing is "The Spirit of Mahongui," presented as the memoir of a French *voyageur* in Canada who is captured by the Iroquois, adopted into an Indian family, and eventually tempted to go to war with them against the French. Here, for the first time in his writings, Remington gives an extended, sympathetic account of Indian life. The Indians themselves are presented as persons of sensitivity and complexity, capable of subtle distinctions and appreciations. In the inlaid tale of a dog's possession by the spirit of a great warrior, he gives an evocative sense of the Indian's relationship to the spirit world as well as to the natural world. This attitude does not appear at all in his earlier works.

Why Remington experienced this apparent change of heart toward the Indian is unclear, but two reasons seem likely. First, as he develops as a writer, he begins to see the degree to which he has previously oversimplified the Indian character. Second, as his own awareness of the vanishing West develops, he comes to see that the Indian is essential to that West, giving to it part of its overall character. That this process is working within him is plain. Some, he says, will scoff at the *voyageur's* tale; "but to those I say, Go to your microbes, your statistics, your volts, and your bicycles, and leave me the truth of other days" (*Crooked Trails,* p. 52). His imagery is as telling as his comment, for he presents the artifacts of technology as being in opposition to the truth of other days.

Two events that were to prove important in Remington's development as artist and author occurred in 1899. The first was an exhibition of Charles Rollo Peters' impressionistic paintings, held at the Union League Club in New York. Here Remington was for the first time exposed to impressionism, a movement that was to play a major rôle in influencing his later paintings (Hassrick, *Frederic Remington,* p. 41). The second event was the publication of *Sundown Leflare.* He had already published one book in 1899, *Stories of Peace and War,* a slender collection of three previously anthologized stories—"The Strange Days That Came to Jimmie Friday," "Joshua Goodenough's Old Letter," and "Chasing a Major-General"—that was apparently intended to capitalize upon American enthusiasm over the Spanish-American War. In contrast to this negligible book, *Sundown Leflare* shows his first clear signs of breaking away from the brief, journalistic pieces of his first three books.

Sundown Leflare is a transitional work. It continues the format of the earlier books in that it is a collection of five short stories published separately in *Harper's Monthly.* It also continues Remington's interest in local color and dialect stories, an interest previously revealed in "The Spirit of Mahongui," and it reflects again his fascination with all that is picturesque. The half-breed Sundown, he writes, is "an exotic, and could never bore a man who had read a little history" (*Sundown Leflare,* p. 51). At the same time, the book demonstrates his emerging skill as a writer of fiction. Though separate and complete in themselves, the stories are unified in time, place, and character, forming a coherent whole that anticipates several of the themes that dominate his last works.

The story line of *Sundown Leflare* is a simple one. A first-person narrator, an Eastern painter clearly meant to be Remington himself, reports a series of conversations with Leflare while on a trip through the West. He first tells of Leflare's acting as interpreter while he tries to write down the story of "The Great Medicine-Horse." He then hears of Leflare's low-key heroism in delivering an order for General Nelson Miles ("How Order Number Six Went Through"), and then he relates the protracted combat between Leflare and Snow-Owl over a woman ("Sundown Leflare's Warm Spot"). Back within the borders of civilization, their conversations continue, telling of Leflare's financial boom and bust in the hands of a tinhorn gambler ("Sundown Leflare's Money") and of his reconciliation of his native faith in Indian medicine with his more recently acquired Roman Catholicism ("Sundown's Higher Self").

Implicit in the stories are several themes that lift the book above its predecessors. One is the growing friendship of the narrator and Leflare. Although the Eastern white man never fully comes to appreciate the full breadth of Indian life, his attitude toward Leflare is far more sympathetic and understanding than anything which appeared in Remington's earlier books. Other themes include the basic vitality of Indian culture; the organic, ecological relationship of the Indian to the natural world; and the failure of the whites to assimilate the Indian into the new West which the white people are creating. Through these themes Remington intensifies his romanticizing of the West, showing how the white man's values and technology are destroying the truth of other days.

The vital life-spirit of Indian culture appears throughout the stories, as Leflare yarns with the narrator about hunting, fighting, and living. This spirit becomes most obvious in the last story, when Leflare contrasts the Indian's life-oriented religion with the death-oriented one of the white man. "Pries' he good peop'," Leflare comments; "all time wan' tak care of me when I die. Well, all right, dees Enjun medicine-man she tak care of me when I was leeve sometime. You s'pose I wan' die all time? No; I wan' leeve; un I got de medicine ober een my teepee—varrie good medicine. Eet tak me troo good many plass where I not geet troo maybeso" (*Sundown Leflare,* pp. 98-99). The basic difference is clear: the Indian is concerned with the immediacy of life, the white man with the future and the hereafter. As Remington later makes explicit, the white man's preoccupation with what lies ahead is the basis of his passion for progress; and that passion, in its turn, creates long-lasting destruction.

More telling is the contrast between the fragmentation of the white man's culture and the organic unity of the Indian's, a contrast which is implicit in Leflare himself. "Sundown was cross-bred, red and white, so he never got mentally in sympathy with either strain of his progenitors" (*Sundown Leflare,* p. 3). Despite the white man's condescension, though, Leflare is far more at home with the Indian way of life than he is with the more civilized one. The Indian's way accepts the presence of nature. It regards the natural world as an ally rather than as an opponent. In a few words, Leflare sums up the Indian's view: "Maybeso white man she don' need medicine. White man she don't 'pear know enough see speeret. Humph! white man can't see wagon-track on de cloud. Enjun he go all over de snow; he lie een de dark; he leeve wid de win' de tunder—well, he leeve all time out on de grass—nighttime—daytime—all de time" (*Sundown Leflare,* p. 100). The white man shuts out the wind and tramples the grass; the Indian makes nature a part of his total existence.

When Remington writes of the interaction of white and Indian, he hits his full stride. By 1899, when *Sundown Leflare* appeared, he was widely recognized as the recorder of a passing era (White, *The Eastern Establishment and the Western Experience,* p. 192). In *Sundown Leflare* he evokes in words the same sense of transition that appeared in his paintings. The old, free West was gone, and the voice of the exploiter was heard throughout the land. Leflare's mixed ancestry is a poignant commentary. So, too, is his ready embracing of the white man's clothing and weaponry: "I was all same Enjun—fringe, bead, long hair—but I was wear de hat. I was hab de bes' pony een de country, un I was hab de firs' breech-loadair een de country. Ah, I was reech!" (*Sundown Leflare,* p. 56). For all his adoption of white ways, though, Leflare remains, like the Indians in general, an alien in the white man's world, a victim ripe for exploitation. When a crooked gambler fleeces him of his profits from a horse trade, he remarks wryly, "Money she no gran' good ting for Enjun man lak for white folk. Enjun she keep de money een hees han' 'bout long she keep de snow een hees han', but I was tell you eet was all he was geet dese day" (*Sundown Leflare,* p. 74). Once the brutal but worthy opponent of the equally worthy soldier, the Indian is now a pathetic figure. He can anglicize his exterior, but he cannot cope with the ways of the whites.

Remington's awareness of the tension between whites and Indians runs throughout the book, for the opening story states the theme. In "The Great Medicine-Horse," the narrator hears of a magical horse that brings peace and plenty to the Absarokes. When it leaves, their fortunes decline. In Lefllare's words, "Dese Enjun have not yet see de medicin'-horse nowday; eef dey was seen heem more, dey see no 'yellow eyes' een dees country." The horse will return, the legend goes on, bringing with it ample buffalo and the defeat of the whites, when the Absaroke give up the white man's ways and return to their old life. "By Gar," rasps Leflare, "I t'ink he not come varrie soon" (*Sundown Leflare,* pp. 20-21). This theme, the incompatibility of Indian and white, develops as the book progresses. Leflare's memorable picture of the white man's coming vividly states the inexorable change:

> Back yondair, een what year you call '80—all same time de white man was hang de oddar white man so fas'—she geet be bad. De buffalo man she was come plenty wid de beeg wagon, was all shoot up de buffalo, was tak all de robe. Den de man come up wid de cow, un de soldier he was stop chasse de Enjun. De Enjun she was set roun' de log pos', un was not wan' be chasse some more—eet was do no good. Den come de railroad; aftar dat bad, all bad. (*Sundown Leflare,* p. 75)

Remington's statement could not be more explicit. The steady advance of the white man's culture, brought first by hunters, then by settlers and soldiers, last and permanently by the railroad, is "bad, all bad." The process that Frederick Jackson Turner looked upon as the most American of all is for Frederic Remington a destructive one. The West is gone, victim of an irreversible conquest masquerading as progress.

The importance of *Sundown Leflare* to Remington's development as a writer was largely lost on his public, and the book had only a lukewarm reception. Perhaps as a result of this reception, he returned to the anthology format in his fifth book, *Men With the Bark On* (1900). This collection is based upon his major pieces of journalism from the Spanish-American War, fleshed out with short stories and essays drawn from the Harper magazines. Despite his return to the simpler format of his earlier books, Remington continues to explore and develop many of the themes of *Sundown Leflare.* In doing so, he creates a bridge between *Sundown Leflare,* a unified collection of short stories, and *John Ermine of the Yellowstone,* his major piece of fiction.

When Sundown Leflare tells his artist acquaintance that life after the coming of the railroad was "bad, all bad," he sets the stage for *Men With the Bark On.* Taking its tone from its epigraph, "Men with the bark on die like the wild animals, unnaturally, unmourned, and even unthought of mostly," the book begins Remington's outright mourning for the old West. He has known, in his mind, that the West he loved was dead; his short stories say as much. In *Men With the Bark On,* he accepts its passing in his heart. The stories make use of the same general subjects found in the early books—hunting, the Indian, the military. Now, though, with his skepticism toward technology confirmed by his experiences in Cuba, Remington sets out to record a new West and to eulogize the old. The new West of which he writes is no longer the rough and ready realm found in his first books. Instead, it is a world dominated by forces greater than the men who claim to control them, the forces of bureaucracy and technology.

"A Failure of Justice," the only story in the book not directly concerned with Indians, hunting, or soldiers, expresses Remington's growing distaste for the modern world. A brief vignette of classic Western chivalry, it records a gambler's defense of the only good woman in a small Western town when she is crudely jollied by a trio of drunken Easterners. The story, of itself, is not extraordinary. It is set apart, though, by Remington's explicit pitting of Eastern ways against Western ways. The trio, he remarks, "had simply applied the low street customs of an Eastern city in a place where customs were low enough, except in the treatment of decent women" (*Men With the Bark On,* p. 80). The pervasive roughness of the town in general is not lost upon him, but the town has an innate regard for womanhood that contrasts tellingly with the boorishness of the more "civilized" Easterners.

A similarly modified view, foreshadowed by *Sundown Leflare,* appears in two stories of Indian life. In the first, "A Sketch by MacNeil," a grizzled frontier scout tells of being trapped in a snowstorm with a group of Crow warriors. Unprepared for a blizzard, the Indians survive by dancing through the night, an activity affording the scout considerable amusement. To Remington, the dance is an act of heroism. The scout's coarse insensitivity to the Indians' dignity expresses the growing indifference of the white man. The second story of Indian life, "The Story of the Dry Leaves," also reveals Remington's growing sympathy for the Indian. This time the Indian is the victim of ecological tragedy, as Ah-we-ah, an Ojibway brave, sees his wife and child starve to death because drought and disease have driven the game away from an already over-hunted territory. Here again is change: the Indian, at one with the elements in *Sundown Leflare,* is now at the mercy of those elements, as helpless to resist a climatic change as he is to resist the white man.

The most extensive statement of Remington's changing views comes in his treatment of his perennially favorite subject, the military man. In the seven stories that deal with the military, he vacillates between two views. He obviously prefers to treat the soldier affectionately, as a Kiplingesque, serio-comic figure who combines lusty fun and professional competence. This is the figure that moves through his early stories. It is also the figure who appears in his treatment of "Soda" Oestreicher, the devoutly loyal trumpeter-orderly of "They Bore a Hand," and in the dedicated men of "L" Troop in "The Honor of the Troop." The company pride of the latter he plainly admires: "Soldiers—by which is meant the real long-service military type —take the government very much as a matter of course; but the number of the regiment, and particularly the letter of their troop, are tangible, comparative things which they are living every day. The feeling is precisely that one has for the Alma Mater, or for the business standing of an old commercial house" (*Men With the Bark On,* p. 26). His sympathy with the men of "L" Troop extends even to his approving their lynching of a scout whose tale-bearing smudges their reputation.

His tendency to treat the soldier as irreverent professional notwithstanding, Remington was far too good a reporter to overlook the evidence confronting him throughout his reporting of the Spanish-American War. His beloved soldiers, the exemplars of individualism and resourcefulness, have been absorbed into a vast, characterless military machine as surely and as inevitably as the Indian has been overwhelmed by the whites. Remington comes to the war with banners flying, wanting to satisfy "a life of longing to see men do the greatest thing which men are called on to do. . . . The creation of things by men in time of peace is of every consequence, but it does not bring forth the tumultuous energy which accompanies the destruction of things by men in war. He who has not seen war only half comprehends the possibilities of his race" (*Men With the Bark On,* pp. 171-72). He leaves the war disillusioned—not by the brutality of warfare, which he has known and can accept, but by the recognition that the wild men of the West, the soldiers and the Indians, "cannot cope with modern war, which dehumanizes them, or modern institutions, which dwarf them, or 'progress,' which passes them by" (White, *Eastern Establishment,* p. 116).

Two things in particular haunt him as he records the war. One is the contamination of the military by amateurs and bureaucrats. The coolly direct competence of the old Army is being supplanted by politics and other irrelevancies. He speaks of this change elsewhere in 1898, in a *Harper's Weekly* squib entitled "Take the Army Out of Politics"; and he continues writing about it in "The War Dreams," wherein a group of servicemen, yearning over dinner before shipping out, tell of their dreams. His ammunition exhausted because of supply delays, an artilleryman uses dead soldiers, then civilians, and at last Congressmen for projectiles. An infantryman finds himself in command of a corps of old men who try to bribe him with money and then with their daughters in order to avoid combat. If wars are going to be run by bureaucrats, Remington implies, the bureaucrats should be on the firing line.

More disturbing than the amateurishness of the Army is the growing dehumanization of warfare itself. Believing that the Army is represented by one man with a rifle, Remington finds that his art "requires me to go down in the road where the human beings are who do these things," and those human beings function best when left to their own devices (*Men With the Bark On,* p. 191). He is confronted, though, by a military machine which puts a premium on massed action and which strives to stamp out individual initiative. The most repellent form of this anti-individualism he finds in the Navy. Of a battleship he writes: "Men stood about in the overpowering blasts of heat . . . men who have succumbed to modern science, which is modern life. Daisies and trees and the play of sunlight mean nothing to these—they know when all three are useful, which is enough" (*Men With the Bark On,* p. 16). Individualism, like the things of nature, has no place in this mechanized world. There is no longer room for a Sergeant Carter Johnson.

Men With the Bark On advances the themes that run through *Sundown Leflare.* In the latter, Remington's emphasis is upon the impact that the white man's technology and ways have had upon the Indian. In the former, he expands his view to embrace the other inhabitants of the West, ruefully observing that even the military is not immune to the ceaseless changes. He observes, too, that the changes involve more than simply the white man's way of life, but that they involve life in general. His first reaction is one of dismay. He deplores what he sees, and he grieves that there is no longer a place for the world that he has known. His second response is a more telling one. He glorifies the old ways and the familiar characters, bathing them in the nostalgic light of romance. In this vanished world, social values are innately proper, inhabitants properly vital. It is a world possessing all of the qualities which he reveres but which he cannot find in his own time. In *Men With the Bark On,* in the guise of journalism, he gives a dual view of life, reporting it as it has become and also as it might be. In *John Ermine of the Yellowstone,* unhampered by the need to report events as observed, he goes on to develop his dual vision, coming at last to the most extended statement of his view of the vanished West.

Remington's development as a writer of fiction reaches its highest point in his novel *John Ermine of the Yellowstone.* Working at the height of his artistic and literary powers, he completes his break with the fragmented format of his previous books and presents a closely knit story of a young man's growth, maturity, and meaningless death. Published in November 1902, the book quickly caught the public eye and sold well. A second printing was called for within a month. Moreover, its theatrical possibilities did not go unnoticed. A stage version, dramatized by Louis Evan Shipman and starring James K. Hackett and Charlotte Walker, opened in Boston in September 1903, and later moved to New York for a moderately successful run (McCracken, *Artist of the Old West,* p. 111).

Despite the merits of the novel as an adventure tale, the real significance of *John Ermine* lies in its presentation of Remington's familiar themes, and it continues the elegiac view of a changing West that appears so strongly in *Men With the Bark On.* As Remington's longest statement of his feelings toward the West, toward progress, and toward humanity, it complements Owen Wister's *The Virginian,* which had been issued by the same publisher half a year earlier. Wister's nameless hero comes to grips with the changing times, wins his Molly, makes his investments, and settles down to a prosperous and fruitful life. Remington's Ermine, in contrast, meets only with failure. In his promising life and wasteful death, he typifies Remington's view of the entire West.

In bald outline, *John Ermine* seems little more than an ordinary adventure yarn. A blond-haired, blue-eyed white boy of Nordic ancestry, Ermine is introduced as a child being reared by a band of Absaroke Indians. His childhood parallels that of the Indian children; he takes part in their play and proves himself to be their equal in strength and ability. As an adolescent, he becomes the ward of Crooked Bear, a white mountain man, who instructs him in the ways of the whites, teaches him English, and gives him a rudimentary education.

After four years with Crooked Bear, Ermine strikes out on his own, determined to become an Army scout. Once accepted by the military, he quickly proves his ability and becomes one of the most respected and sought-after of the scouts, even though he remains an object of some bewilderment to the white soldiers. Disaster comes when he falls in love with Katherine Searles, the frigidly Easternized daughter of the commandant. Misled by her fashionable coquetries, he proposes marriage to her and accepts his inevitable rejection. But he cannot accept the abuse heaped upon him by Lieutenant Butler, Katherine's fiancé, and by the other officers. He shoots Butler in the arm and flees into the hills, where he attempts to resume his life as an Indian. But this he cannot do. When he returns to the Army camp intending to kill Butler, he is himself shot in the back by one of the other scouts whom he had angered months before.

Remington's major theme is once again the conflict of two cultures, including their basic incompatibility, and the helplessness of the more primitive one in the face of the steady advance of the more technologically adept one. On the one hand, Katherine Searles and the officers' wives, with their veneer of Eastern mores, represent contemporary technological society. On the other hand Ermine embodies all that is good in primitive society. He is "evolved from a race, which . . . got its yellow hair, fair skin, and blue eyes amid the fjords, forests, rocks, and ice-floes of the north of Europe" (*John Ermine,* 1968 ed., p. 22). White though he is, Ermine in his primitiveness is an integral part of the Western scene. This state of harmony is explicit in the description of Ermine and a fellow scout, a Crow, on the trail:

> These two figures, crawling, sliding, turning, and twisting through the sunlight on the rugged mountains, were grotesque but harmonious. America will never produce their like again. Her wheels will turn and her chimneys smoke, and the things she makes will be carried around the world in ships, but she never can make two figures which will bear even a remote resemblance to Wolf-Voice and John Ermine. The wheels and chim-

> neys and the white men have crowded them off the earth. (*John Ermine,* pp. 87-88)

Organically right and admirable though the primitive may be, he is the one who must yield when the primitive and the modern meet.

Ermine's talents flourish in the open naturalness of military life. The old Army takes him on his merits and his competence, and for this reason he is accepted as a scout. When Eastern ways are imposed upon the West, however, competence is not enough. A new hypocrisy overshadows the manly openness of the old West. "I know you think I am a dog," Ermine blurts out:

> I know Miss Searles thinks I belong in the corral with the mules; but, by G--, you did not think I was a dog when the Sioux had your wagon-train surrounded and your soldiers buffaloed. . . . You did not think I was a dog when I kept you all from freezing to death last winter; but here among the huts and the women I am a dog. I tell you now that I do not understand such men as you are. You have two hearts: one is red and the other is blue; and you feel with the one that best suits you at the time. (*John Ermine,* pp. 235-36)

The subtle, devious ways of the East have no place in the West, but they are there, brought by the white man's civilization and forcing a revision of the older and honorable values.

Remington makes it clear throughout the novel that he is speaking of more than merely whites and Indians. He gives to Ermine all of the attributes of the white man's world: blond hair, blue eyes, white skin, and the promise of acceptance. The whites, Crooked Bear tells Ermine, "will come in numbers as great as the grasshoppers, but you will not care; you are a white man" (*John Ermine,* p. 76). These attributes, however, are of themselves not enough to save him. His genetic inheritance is European, but his cultural inheritance is Indian. When the crisis comes, his primitive traits, established by his upbringing and reinforced by his treatment at the hands of the whites, prove stronger than his racial ties. "All the patient training of Crooked Bear, all the humanizing influence of white association, all softening moods . . . were blown from the fugitive as though carried on a wind; he was a shellfish-eating cave-dweller, with a Springfield, a knife, and a revolver. He had ceased to think in English, and muttered to himself in Absaroke" (*John Ermine,* pp. 268-69). The primitive virtues, once so vital to the West, again assert themselves, this time working against Ermine. He is a product of the old West, and he dies because he is what he is.

John Ermine stands alone among Remington's books. In it, he works with familiar materials—the West, the Indians, the military—but he molds them into a tellingly different pattern. The impersonal and dehumanizing qualities of the present that so disturbed him in Cuba have now penetrated to the West of his memories. Where once he found in the West unlimited opportunity for the individual to live with direct and open dealings, he now finds arbitrary, unfeeling, and institutionalized restrictions. No longer does the West judge a person's life on the basis of his achievements; instead, it judges by standards imposed from the outside. The result is tragedy, a far different result from the idyllic ending of *The Virginian.* Wister's eponymous hero yields to the new ways, becomes a modern Westerner, and is assimilated into the new world. John Ermine, in contrast, cannot do these things and does not yield. A man of the West by nature and training, he clings to the values that his life has shown him are good, and he dies when the world changes about him.

The Way of an Indian, published in 1906, was Remington's last book. With it, he rounds out the chronicle of the vanishing West that he began with *Sundown Leflare* and developed in *John*

Ermine. The former, with its account of a halfbreed scout's attempts to endure in a world not his own, sets the scene, establishing the basic incompatibility of the white man's ways with those of the Indian. *John Ermine* enlarges that scope to encompass primitive life, or the natural life, in general. Though he is a white man, Ermine is also natural man, and he finds himself in a world that has no place for him. *The Way of an Indian* finishes the development of Remington's view of the West. Focusing upon a Cheyenne brave, the book relates the Indian's growth to maturity in his own world and his destruction in the white man's world.

Despite its significance in the body of Remington's work, *The Way of an Indian* is comparatively little known. It was featured as a serial in *Cosmopolitan* and drew an admiring letter from Theodore Roosevelt (Remington papers, February 20, 1906). Following its publication in book form, though, it attracted little attention. None of the studies of Remington to date considers it, and it has not yet been reprinted. Remington himself, however, thought highly of the book. In a 1907 interview, he cited it, with *Pony Tracks* and *Crooked Trails,* as "done with the deliberate view of educating men and women, who knew not the West, up to a certain standard of appreciation for its beauties, its fascinations, its intrinsic worth" (Maxwell, "Frederic Remington, Most Typical of American Artists," p. 405). Despite this intention, the book did not do well. Its pervasive somberness and its lack of a wholly attractive hero seem to have overshadowed its merits.

Like *John Ermine, The Way of an Indian* follows the traditional model of the story of maturation. It tells of White Otter, a young Cheyenne, as he strives for distinction within his tribe. In the course of this striving, he undergoes a solitary medicine ordeal, converses with the spirits of nature, and finds his spiritual emblem in the little brown bat. With the bat to guide him, he goes forth to prove himself. He tests the bat's medicine against the counsel of the gray spider and the gray wolf; then he easily steals several Absaroke ponies, kills and scalps an Absaroke brave, and returns to his village in triumph, a proved warrior.

Now the equal of any of the men of the tribe, he takes as his warrior's name Ho-to-kee-mat-sin, or The Bat, and goes on to greater exploits. While The Bat is on a hunting expedition, he encounters a white trader's caravan, covets one of the trader's firearms, and strikes a bargain. When the trader reneges on the deal, The Bat steals the trader's stock of horses, confronts him with his duplicity before the tribal council, and returns the horses in exchange for the white man's rifle, a weapon far superior to the smoothbore of the original bargain.

Triumph follows triumph as The Bat matures. He finds the woman he wants for his wife, persuades her to abandon her husband, a French trader, and returns with her to his tribe. In a skirmish with a group of white beaver hunters, he establishes his tactical skill by isolating them from food and water and by waiting for their inevitable death from heat and thirst. His prowess in these and similar encounters makes him the logical successor to the tribe's medicine man and eventually wins him the rank of a sub-chief, whereupon he assumes the name of Fire Eater.

Times change, and the aging Fire Eater finds himself and his tribe more and more hemmed in by encroaching whites: "The talking-wires and the fire wagon found their way, and the white hunters slew the buffalo of the Indians by millions, for their hides" (*Way of an Indian,* p. 197). His medicine emblem, the brown bat, is powerless against the white man's technology and weaponry. Although he wins an occasional clash, as when he and his warriors ruthlessly wipe out a cavalry patrol, it is plain that the day of the Indian is waning. The end comes abruptly, in a night cavalry attack upon Fire Eater's village that is singularly reminiscent of the Wounded Knee incident.

When Fire Eater and the scattered survivors regroup in the mountains, he discovers that his medicine bag, with the bat, has been destroyed in the battle. He is spiritually defenseless. The book ends with Fire Eater, overwhelmed by the loss of his medicine, by the destruction of his people, and by the death of his youngest son, sitting alone, naked and unarmed, stoically awaiting death and the prospects of a better life. "He wanted to go to the spirit-land where the Cheyennes of his home and youth were at peace in warm valleys, talking and eating" (*Way of an Indian,* p. 252). A lifetime has ended for Fire Eater, just as it has ended for the Indian and the unfettered West.

Remington's own pairing of *The Way of an Indian* with *Pony Tracks* is unwittingly revealing, for it tells much about his development since 1895. In one of the stories in *Pony Tracks,* "The Sioux Outbreak in South Dakota," he writes as a young man, and bitterly regrets having missed the "Battle" of Wounded Knee with its triumph of military might over primitive arms. Now, a decade later, he uses the circumstances of the battle to tell a different story, that of the white man's overrunning the Indian and of his destroying all that is vital and natural in the West. What was at first a relatively harmless scattering of whites becomes a ceaseless stream of encroachers, indifferent to the richness of Indian life: "The little bands of traders and beaver-men . . . were succeeded by immense trains of wagons, drawn by the white man's buffalo. The trains wound endlessly toward the setting sun—paying no heed to the Indians" (*Way of an Indian,* p. 194). Seen in the context of *Sundown Leflare* and *John Ermine, The Way of an Indian* becomes Remington's final statement. To those who will listen, as his comment to Perriton Maxwell makes explicit, he can teach a valuable lesson; to those who will not, he says no more. Although he continued painting and sculpture until his death in 1909, he published nothing else. His silence is as poignantly eloquent as any polemic that he might have written.

Frederic Remington will never be hailed as a major American author. His lasting reputation will quite properly come from his paintings and bronzes, for here he was the innovator. In his lifetime, he was recognized as "one of the few men in this country who has created new conditions in our art; and must be reckoned with as one of the revolutionary figures in our art history" (quoted in McCracken, *Artist of the Old West,* p. 118). Even as he was creating new conditions for pictorial art, however, he was quietly advancing the prominence of the American West in literature. Bringing an artist's eye to literature, he contributed a respect for color and authenticity to the developing literature of the West. What is still more important, his writings stand as valuable documents for the student of the American people's developing attitude toward the West.

Throughout his writings, he articulates a highly personal system of values, embracing a respect for individualism, professional competence, the natural world, and the primitive. These values remain constant even if the way in which he applies them changes somewhat, as his shifting view of the Indian illustrates. As he states these values, he speaks to the American people at a time when they themselves were trying to come to grips with the tensions between the rural past and the increasingly urban present. Speaking to Americans in an era when they were rediscovering the natural world and looking to it as a cure for the ills of city life, he puts forth a view of existence very similar to that of the strenuous life advocated by his friend Theodore Roosevelt. In a lifetime that saw the coming of the national park system, of the fresh-air camp for urban youngsters, and of the Boy Scouts of America, Remington consistently speaks for the rugged life of the out-of-doors, whether in the North Woods of Canada or the Great Plains of the United States.

As he does this, he communicates to the American people a second sense important to the times, a sense that the West is a distinct region, unique on the American continent. Because it is distinctive, it calls for a way of life peculiar to its environs. This is a total way of life, which requires a set of attitudes and assumptions far different from those called for by other regions. The individual who comes to the West, Remington says, must surrender himself totally to the physical and social adaptations that are required. He speaks from experience. The techniques of farming that he knew in New York had no place in Kansas; and, although his high-spirited burning of the Plum Grove, Kansas, schoolhouse did not go unavenged, the penalty was significantly lighter than it might have been in Ogdensburg, New York (Taft, *Artists and Illustrators of the Old West,* pp. 209-10). The requirements of Western life, and the social values that evolve from them, are different from—and in some ways superior to—those of other regions. The person who would move from region to region must recognize the distinctiveness of each and must be prepared to comply with its demands.

Remington's third and most important achievement as an author is to articulate for his readers the poignant sense of loss that he associates with the West's passing from a state of nature to one of civilization. He gives no sign that he knew the writings and theories of his contemporary, the historian Frederick Jackson Turner, but his own writings parallel Turner's in spirit and essence. He staunchly believes in the inherent worth of the West and in its superiority to the East. Remington came to the West as an Easterner seeking his fortune, fresh from Yale University and its football team. Wealth evaded him, but he found instead a coherent pattern of life that gave him a sense of human destiny. He valued this knowledge and recognized that it would be valuable to others. He also recognized that others would not be able to experience the life that he had known on the Western frontier. The West was fading, soon to vanish completely, when Remington first saw it. Acknowledging this rapid transition, he strives in his writings to recreate the Western experience for those who would never taste it for themselves. As he writes of soldiers and Indians, cowboys and hunters, he attempts to capture the vitality of the West in a way that will outlive his ink and paper.

As he tries to record in print the immensity of the nation's loss, he comes to recognize that the task is hopeless. He begins as a reporter, recording humorously but factually the good life. He ends as a saddened and embittered commentator, writing of the destruction of the West by the new gods of the twentieth century, progress and property. Inherent in what the modern American calls progress he sees still further problems: standardization of persons and products replacing vital individualism; the arbitrary dictates of the railroad timetable supplanting human initiative and discretion; the rules of an impersonal and inflexible justice, dictated by Eastern courts, taking precedence over the openness of person-to-person dealings. These are the artifacts of modern man, who comes West to make the region over in his own image, rather than to adapt himself to its requirements. In the path of the American drive for progress, the old, human ways of the West have no chance for survival. Remington comes slowly to this recognition, and his final admission of it is painful.

He states his melancholic conclusions in his "Few Words From Mr. Remington," published in 1905. He returns to the theme again in 1907, when he remarks: "I have no interest whatever in the industrial West of to-day—no more interest than I have in the agriculture of East Prussia or the coal mines of Wales. My West passed utterly out of existence so long ago as to make it merely a dream. It put on its hat, took up its blankets and marched off the board; the curtain came down and a new act was in progress" (Maxwell, "Frederic Remington," p. 407). This sense of loss is what he ultimately conveys in his writings. There once was a time when life was free and natural. Modern man, blundering after material things, has trampled over that natural life. He has crushed it into dust and has replaced it with the characterless monuments of his progress. The life that was destroyed was a good one, Remington tells his readers. But it has been irretrievably lost, and America is the worse for its going.

As a participant in the mythologizing of the American West, Frederic Remington has chiefly been studied as a pictorial artist. His associations with Owen Wister and Theodore Roosevelt have been explored, as have his affection for the military and his yearning for armed combat. He is also worthy of extended study as an author, however, for his written works contribute almost as much to modern America's sense of the West as do his paintings and sculptures. By any objective literary standard he remains a minor author. But he is significant as an observer of a turbulent time and as an author who invested his writings with the same perceptive vision that invigorates his best oils. John Ermine, Sundown Leflare, and the hundreds of faceless United States soldiers who move through his books are memorable creations. They are also useful creations, for Remington the author is also Remington the historian. In his books, as in his paintings, he gives to the student of American life and literature a sense of the rich variety of the old West and of its contributions to national life. William A. Coffin wrote in 1892 that "People have formed their conceptions of what the Far-Western life is like, more from what they have seen in Mr. Remington's pictures than from any other source" ("American Illustrations of To-day," p. 348). Of Remington's writings it may be said that here, too, he spoke to Americans. He spoke for the West—as it was, and as it should have been.

Selected Bibliography

The Remington Papers are in the Remington Art Museum, Ogdensburg, New York, and the St. Lawrence University Library, Canton, New York.

Books by Remington

Pony Tracks. New York: Harper, 1895. Rpt. University of Oklahoma Press, 1961.

A Rogers Ranger in the French and Indian War. New York: Harper, 1897.

Crooked Trails. New York: Harper, 1898. Rpt. Books for Libraries Press, 1969.

Stories of Peace and War. New York: Harper, 1899. Rpt. Books for Libraries Press, 1970.

Sundown Leflare. New York: Harper, 1899.

Men With the Bark On. New York: Harper, 1900.

John Ermine of the Yellowstone. New York: Macmillan, 1902. Rpt. Gregg Press, 1968.

The Way of an Indian. New York: Fox Duffield, 1906.

Articles and Stories by Remington

Short works collected in book form are not included in this listing.

"Coursing Rabbits on the Plains." *Outing,* 10 (May 1887) , 111-21.

"A Peccary Hunt in Northern Mexico." *Harper's Weekly,* 32 (Dec. 1, 1888) , 915.

"Horses of the Plains." *Century,* 37 (January 1889) , 332-43.

"A Scout with the Buffalo-Soldiers." *Century,* 37 (April 1889) , 899-912.

"On the Indian Reservations." *Century,* 38 (July 1889) , 394-405.

"Artist Wanderings Among the Cheyennes." *Century,* 38 (August 1889), 536-45.

"Two Gallant Young Cavalrymen." *Harper's Weekly,* 34 (March 22, 1890), 219.

"The Art of War and Newspaper Men." *Harper's Weekly,* 34 (Dec. 6, 1890), 947.

"Indians as Irregular Cavalry." *Harper's Weekly,* 34 (Dec. 27, 1890), 1004-06.

"General Miles's Review of the Mexican Army." *Harper's Weekly,* 35 (July 4, 1891), 495.

"A Day with the Seventh Regiment." *Harper's Weekly,* 35 (July 18, 1891), 536-38.

"Training Cavalry Horses to Jump Obstacles." *Harper's Weekly,* 35 (Sept. 19, 1891), 710-11.

"Coolies Coaling a Ward Liner—Havana." *Harper's Weekly,* 35 (Nov. 7, 1891), 881.

"The Galloping Sixth." *Harper's Weekly,* 36 (Jan. 16, 1892), 57-58.

"An Appeal for Justice." *Harper's Weekly,* 36 (July 9, 1892), 654-55.

"Buffalo Bill in London." *Harper's Weekly,* 36 (Sept. 3, 1892), 847.

"Military Athletics at Aldershot." *Harper's Weekly,* 36 (Sept. 10, 1892), 882.

"The Uprising in Chihuahua." *Harper's Weekly,* 37 (May 6, 1893), 419.

"The Advance-Guard, or the Military Sacrifice." *Harper's Weekly,* 37 (Sept. 16, 1893), 886.

"A Gallop Through the Midway." *Harper's Weekly,* 37 (Oct. 7, 1893), 963.

" 'Toro, Toro!' " *Harper's Weekly,* 37 (Oct. 7, 1893), 963.

"The Rebellion in Northern Mexico." *Harper's Weekly,* 37 (Dec. 30, 1893), 1247.

"Julian Ralph." *Harper's Weekly,* 38 (Feb. 24, 1894), 179.

"A Rodeo at Los Ojos." *Harper's New Monthly Magazine,* 88 (March 1894), 515-28.

"Troop A Athletics." *Harper's Weekly,* 38 (March 3, 1894), 210.

"Troop A with the Dust On." *Harper's Weekly,* 38 (July 7, 1894), 631-33.

"Chicago Under the Mob." *Harper's Weekly,* 38 (July 21, 1894), 680-81.

"Chicago Under the Law." *Harper's Weekly,* 38 (July 28, 1894), 703.

"The Withdrawal of the U.S. Troops." *Harper's Weekly,* 38 (Aug. 11, 1894), 748.

"A New Infantry Equipment." *Harper's Weekly,* 38 (Sept. 22, 1894), 905.

"Winter Shooting on the Gulf Coast of Florida." *Harper's Weekly,* 39 (May 11, 1895), 451.

"A Cosmopolitan—Mr. Poultney Bigelow." *Harper's Weekly,* 39 (July 20, 1895), 688.

"With the Guns." *Harper's Weekly,* 39 (Aug. 17, 1895), 771.

"Getting Hunters in Horse-Show Form." *Harper's Weekly,* 39 (Nov. 16, 1895), 1088.

"A Practice March in Texas." *Harper's Weekly,* 40 (Jan. 4, 1896), 15.

"Squadron A's Games." *Harper's Weekly,* 40 (March 28, 1896), 295.

"A New Idea for Soldiers." *Harper's Weekly,* 40 (May 2, 1896), 442.

"Hasty-Intrenchment Drill." *Harper's Weekly,* 40 (Aug. 8, 1896), 788.

"Uprising of the Yaqui Indians—Yaqui Warriors in Retreat." *Harper's Weekly,* 40 (Aug. 29, 1896), 857.

"Vagabonding with the Tenth Horse." *Cosmopolitan,* 22 (Feb. 1897), 347-54.

"An Interesting Detail." *Harper's Weekly,* 42 (Jan. 8, 1898), 43.

"The Training of Cavalry." *Harper's Weekly,* 42 (April 2, 1898), 321.

"Wigwags From the Blockade." *Harpers' Weekly,* 42 (May 14, 1898), 462.

"Soldiers Who Cry." *Harper's Weekly,* 42 (May 21, 1898), 502.

"Bring the Fifth Corps North." *Harper's Weekly,* 42 (Aug. 13, 1898), 795.

"Colonel Roosevelt's Pride." *Harper's Weekly,* 42 (Aug. 27, 1898), 848.

"Take the Army Out of Politics." *Harper's Weekly,* 42 (Oct. 15, 1898), 1022.

"How the Horses Died." *Harper's Weekly,* 43 (July 15, 1899), 700.

"Mountain Lions in Yellowstone Park." *Collier's,* 24 (March 17, 1900), 14.

"A Gallant American Officer." *Collier's,* 25 (April 7, 1900), 9.

"A Shotgun Episode." *Outing,* 36 (May 1900), 116-19.

"How a Trout Broke a Friendship." *Outing,* 36 (Sept. 1900), 651-52.

"Natchez's Pass." *Harper's New Monthly Magazine,* 102 (Feb. 1901), 437-43.

"Billy's Tearless Woe." *McClure's,* 16 (March 1901), 455-59.

"How the Worm Turned." *Collier's,* 27 (May 4, 1901), 12.

"A Desert Romance—a Tale of the Southwest." *Century,* 63 (Feb. 1902), 522-30.

"The Strategy of the Blanket Pony." *Collier's,* 28 (Feb. 1, 1902), 14-15.

"A Few Words from Mr. Remington." *Collier's,* 34 (March 18, 1905), 16.

"Jefferson as a Painter." *Harper's Weekly,* 49 (May 13, 1905), 684-85.

Collections

Allen, Douglas, ed. *Frederic Remington and the Spanish-American War.* New York: Crown, 1971.

———. *Frederic Remington's Own Outdoors.* New York: Dial, 1964.

McCracken, Harold, ed. *Frederic Remington's Own West.* New York: Dial, 1960.

Vorpahl, Ben Merchant. *My Dear Wister: The Frederic Remington-Owen Wister Letters.* Palo Alto: American West, 1972.

Bibliographies

Allen, E. Douglas. "Frederic Remington—Author and Illustrator—A List of His Contributions to American Periodicals." *Bulletin of the New York Public Library,* 49 (Dec. 1945) , 895-912.

Dykes, Jeff C. "Tentative Bibliographic Check Lists of Western Illustrators: XXVI., Frederic Remington (1861-1909) ." *American Book Collector,* 16 (Nov.-Dec. 1965; Jan.-April 1966) , 20-31, 22-31, 26-31, 34-39, 21-27, 23-25.

Selected Secondary Works

Alter, Judith. "Frederic Remington's Major Novel: *John Ermine.*" *Southwestern American Literature,* 2 (Spring 1972) , 42-46.

———. "The Western Myth in American Painting and Fiction of the Late 19th and Early 20th Centuries." Unpublished Doctoral Dissertation, Texas Christian University, 1970.

Barnes, James. "Frederic Remington—Sculptor." *Collier's,* 34 (March 18, 1905) , 21.

Bigelow, Poultney. "Frederic Remington; with Extracts from Unpublished Letters." *The Quarterly of the New York Historical Association,* 10 (Jan. 1929) , 45-52.

———. *Seventy Summers.* New York: Longmans, Green, 1925.

Brown, Myra Lockwood, and Robert Taft. "Painter of the Rip-Roaring West." *Country Gentleman,* 117 (Sept. 1947) , 16-17, 79-80.

Coffin, William A. "American Illustration of To-day." *Scribner's Magazine,* 11 (March 1892) , 333-49.

Cortissoz, Royal. *American Artists.* New York: Scribner, 1923.

Crooker, Orin Edson. "A Page from the Boyhood of Frederic Remington." *Collier's,* 45 (Sept. 17, 1910), 28.

Davis, Charles Belmont, ed. *Adventures and Letters of Richard Harding Davis.* New York: Scribner, 1917.

———. "Remington—The Man and His Work." *Collier's,* 34 (March 18, 1905), 15.

Dykes, Jeff C. "Frederic Remington—Western Historian." *American Book Collector,* 9 (April 1959), 4-8.

Edgerton, Giles. "Frederic Remington, Painter and Sculptor." *Craftsman,* 15 (March 1909), 658-70.

Erisman, Fred. "Frederic Remington: the Artist as Local Colorist." *South Dakota Review,* 12 (Winter 1974-75), 76-88.

"Frederic Remington—A Painter of the Vanishing West." *Current Literature,* 43 (Nov. 1907), 521-25.

Garland, Hamlin. *Crumbling Idols.* Chicago: Stone and Kimball, 1894.

———. *Roadside Meetings.* New York: Macmillan, 1930.

Hassrick, Peter H. *Frederic Remington.* New York: Abrams, 1973.

———. "Remington in the Southwest." *Southwestern Historical Quarterly,* 76 (Jan. 1973), 297-314.

Hough, Emerson. "Wild West Faking." *Collier's,* 42 (Dec. 19, 1908), 18-19, 22.

Hough, Nellie. "Remington at Twenty-three." *International Studio,* 76 (Feb. 1923), 413-15.

de Kay, Charles. "A Painter of the West: Frederic Remington and His Work." *Harper's Weekly,* 54 (Jan. 8, 1910), 14-15, 38.

McCracken, Harold. *Frederic Remington: Artist of the Old West.* Philadelphia: Lippincott, 1947.

———. *The Frederic Remington Book: A Pictorial History of the West.* Garden City: Doubleday, 1966.

McKown, Robin. *Painter of the Wild West, Frederic Remington.* New York: Messner, 1959.

Marden, Orison S. *Little Visits with Great Americans.* New York: Success, 1905.

Maxwell, Perriton. "Frederic Remington, Most Typical of American Artists." *Pearson's,* 18 (Oct. 1907), 395-407.

Parkman, Francis. *Letters of Francis Parkman.* Ed. Wilbur R. Jacobs. Norman: University of Oklahoma Press, 1960.

Ralph, Julian. "Frederic Remington." *Harper's Weekly,* 39 (July 20, 1895), 688.

Roosevelt, Theodore. *Letters of Theodore Roosevelt,* ed. Elting E. Morison, *et al.* Cambridge: Harvard University Press, 1951.

Rush, N. Orwin. "Frederic Remington and Owen Wister: The Story of a Friendship, 1893-1909." *Probing the American West: Papers from the Santa Fe Conference.* Ed. K. Ross Toole, *et al.* Santa Fe: Museum of New Mexico, 1962. Pp. 148-57.

Taft, Robert. *Artists and Illustrators of the Old West, 1850-1900.* New York: Scribner, 1953.

Thomas, Augustus. *The Print of My Remembrance.* New York: Scribner, 1922.

———. "Recollections of Frederic Remington." *Century,* 86 (July 1913), 354-61.

White, G. Edward. *The Eastern Establishment and the Western Experience: The West of Frederic Remington, Theodore Roosevelt, and Owen Wister.* Yale Publications in American Studies, 14. New Haven: Yale University Press, 1968.

Wildman, Edwin. "Frederic Remington, the Man." *Outing,* 41 (March 1903), 712-16.

Wister, Owen. "Preface." *Members of the Family.* New York: Macmillan, 1911.